ADDENDA

CHARLES CARUSO

Addenda   2

IT'S EASY WHEN YOU HAVE NO CHOICE

THIS UNRULY WORLD

ACTIVITY

Most human activity is aimed at avoiding loneliness.

BIOPSIES

First the biopsy, then the autopsy.

BRIDE

Altar ego

BRIGADOONS

Everyone has a Brigadoon somewhere.

BUTTERFLIES

How would a butterfly collector like to be caught in a net, impaled on a sharp instrument, then pressed into someone's grimy catalogue?

CHUCKLES
The first chuckle means our morning depression is over.

CONDIMENTS
Some people are mustard, some mayonnaisse.
Some people are coffee, some tea.
Some people look like they've never been brought to a boil.

CYNICS
A sinecure will cure a cynic.

CLAQUES
A claque is a clique that claps.

CLASS
People who are always talking about 'class' never have any.

CLOTHES
Dirty clothes are warmer.

DAY

Another day, another dolor.

DEATH

Death isn't suffering. Death is the end of suffering.

DELAY

Delay is doom to the petitioner.

DOGS

The world isn't going to the dogs. The dogs have had it all along.

DOING

Arrange by doing. As you do, the arrangement appears.

EARTH

One day we're on top of the earth. Next day the earth is on top of us.

ELITE
The effete elite live chiefly in the east.

ENDEAVOR
Most human endeavor is aimed at making money.
The rest is devoted to finding love. After a while,
we think less about love and more about dinner.

ESTIMATE
Never underestimate human potential for error or treachery.

FAMILIARITY
Familiarity breeds content.

A GOOD DAY
A good day is getting to bed in one piece.

HAPPY

We only recognize our happiest years when they're past.

HOME

An apartment is not a home. A house is a home.

HOME TRUTHS

People who tell home truths should stay home.

HUMANS

They can fly to the moon and dance 'Swan Lake,' as all the while a foul package is forming in their gut.

HUMORISTS

A humorist is always grinding an axiom.

HUNTING

A true hunter would take a knife and enter a thicket where a wild boar lives and battle it out with him. No blind, no camouflage. Just him and the boar. Best man wins.

INFANT

At the heart of our tenderness for an infant is pity.

LIARS

Never give a liar an out by putting words in his mouth.
Let him tell his shabby story and entrap himself.

LIONS AND LAMBS

The lion lies down with the lamb only when the lamb is safely inside him.

LOOKS

Good looks are an asset for a woman but trouble for a man.

LOOPS

If you're outside the loop, you may soon be outside the door.

PEANUT BUTTER
Peanut butter is the caviar of the poor.

PUNCTUATION
A light vertical stroke turns a deathly x into a celestial *

NICE
Some guys finish last and they're not even nice.

NOSTALGIA
Someone else's nostalgia is so boring.
Descriptions of his illnesses too.

PHASES
From bright to blight
From revolutionary to revolting
From important to impotent.

POISE
The truest test of poise is how you act when your hat blows off
-- or when you're stood up.

SAD/MAD
Don't get sad, get mad. Do something! *Even if it's wrong.*

WORLD'S PROBLEMS
All the world's problems fade into insignificance next to a broken toilet.

PHOTOGRAPHS
People often don't like photographs of themselves because they have an idealized vision of themselves that usually bears little resemblance to reality.

PROGRESSION
Little by little we get it together and little by little it falls apart.

REACTIONS
Everyone's first reaction to everything: What's in it for me?

RESPONSIBILITY
The one in the seat gets the heat, the fame or the blame.

ROLES

We start as Hamlet and end as Polonius.

RUNS

You have your run and then you're done.

SEMI-COLONS

A semi-colon is a comma with a head on its shoulders.

SKYLINE

Ugly new Manhattan buildings: Eyescrapers.

SLIPS

A slip of the lip can sink a quip.

SNEERS

A sneer is the sign of a broken heart.

SUNSHINE

You never know how many people there are in the world until the sun comes out.

THE THREE WISE MEN

Where were the Three Wise Men when he needed them?

TROUBLES

Most of the troubles of the world would have been avoided if people had just stayed home --if Napoleon hadn't gone to Russia, if Lincoln hadn't gone to the theater, if Kennedy hadn't gone to Dallas.

WINNING

We all believe that we will win in the end --- that some day, somehow we will master events and make everything right. This is what keeps us going.

A MATTER OF WIFE AND DEBT

LOVE AND SEX

ABUSE

A man can accept a lot of abuse from a woman with a good figure.

ADULTERY

The first rule in adultery, as in espionage, is to deny everything.

COPULATION

We copulate to populate.

BED

Man does not live by bed alone.

If you're laughing in bed, you're not really aroused.
Sex is a serious business.

BLOOD AND SEMEN

Blood is thicker than semen. Family ties outlast the sexual.

CHEATING

The strongest ally a dissembling husband or wife has is the deceived mate who desperately wants to believe the cheater's story.

CONFESSION

Confession may be good for the soul but it's hard on a marriage.

CONNECTIONS

You really connect with only two or three people in your life.

COURTSHIP

From bedding to wedding.

DAYS

We should treat people we love as if every day were their last.

DEBT

The wages of sin are debt.

DESIRE

A man's desire for a woman was the beginning of civilization.

Desire is more important for a man than a woman
because a man can't fake sex.

Where a man's eye lingers on a women's body, his hand yearns to follow.

DESTITUTE

A destitute prostitute is a poor whore.

DIVORCE

The seeds of divorce are sown long before the wedding.

The last thing a divorced man will admit is how much he misses his wife.

ECONOMICS

There has been an economic element in the sexual
relationship since the beginning of time.

FACES
A man never really sees his wife's face until he sees her
sitting across a table next to her lawyer.

FANTASIES
Someone who has been without sex for a while takes
a little time to switch from a fantasy lover to a real one.

FLAWS
Before you bemoan the supposed flaws of your lady friend,
consider that without them she may have made a better deal.

FOOLS
A fool and his honey are soon parted.

FUTILITY
Locking the bedroom door after your whore is stolen.

GIFTS
Anything given with love is worth more than diamonds.

People don't see gifts as objects. They see them as tokens of love.

HAIR
If a girl on the street likes you, she immediately begins fussing with her hair.

HAPPY
To make a woman happy lie in her arms all night.

HONOR
When a man 'defends a woman's honor', he's really defending his own.

LIBERATION
A liberated women is one who helps with the check.

LIFE AND DEATH
Love is a matter of life and death:
If someone loves us, they will feed us when we're hungry, shelter us when we're homeless, nurse us when we're sick, amuse us when we're sad.

LOVE

We love what we loved. We love now what we loved before.

Everyone has a certain measure of love to give. If the love object is removed, the love soon transfers to another.

LOVE AND MONEY

Money is a surer thing than love. Love loses interest, but money *draws* interest.

LOVE AND WORK

When your love life is down, concentrate on your work life. When your work life is down, concentrate on your love life.

LOVE SONGS

Men write most of the long songs because women are too practical to think up that drivel.

LOVING

Loving is giving. As long as you keep giving, you'll keep living.

MATES
You can tell everything about people by their choice of mates.

MARRIAGE
First you settle down, then you settle up.

You can tell the fragility of a friend's marriage by the number of times he says 'I love you' on the phone.

Most men marry just to get a good night's sleep.

MOMS AND MOTHERS
After a divorce, how soon 'Mom' become 'your mother.'

NATURE'S WAY
Sex is nature's way of persuading men to spend
 their best years supporting strangers.

ORGASMS
An orgasm is a surrender. Most people don't surrender easily.

OVERSEXED
Being married to an oversexed woman is penile servitude.

PANTS
Women usually have an eye out for the bulge in a man's pants -- his wallet, that is.

PARENTS
We don't appreciate our parents until they're gone.

PERCENTAGES
Fifty percent of all marriages fail. If fifty percent of all planes crashed would we get on one?

PROMISCUOUS
New face, new fanny.

PURSUIT
The best way to get rid of a pursuing woman is to marry her.

SEX
Sex is a simple matter of appendages and apertures.

Sex is undignified.

SEX AND FOOD

Food is better than sex because the only relationship you have to worry about is the one between knife and fork.

Sex is like dinner. You'd prefer to have it with someone you like. But if you're hungry enough, you'll have it with anyone -- even yourself.

TENDER
Love is the tender trap all right -- legal tender.

WOMAN
A women is a package: character, brains, looks -- face, hair, top, bottom and legs. Character is by far the most important.

A pretty woman is pretty in a torn undershirt.

A plain one is plain in a thousand-dollar gown.

A woman is surrounded by an electrical field that says
either Come In or Stay Out.

WOMEN
Women liked to be looked at but not stared at.

WOMEN AND MEN
Women get together and say: Let's have a patio picnic.
I'll bring my potato salad, you bring your spinach quiche and
there'll be hotdogs and balloons for the kids.
Men get together and say: Let's build a bigger bomb.

WOMEN: ANOTHER VIEW
Women shouldn't have combat roles in the military -- they're too cruel.

EVERYONE LAUGHS AT THE BOSS'S JOKES

WORK AND MONEY

ANSWERING
In an age of answering machines, opportunity doesn't knock. It blinks.

DECOR
A picture crooked on the wall foretells a company's imminent fall.

DESPAIR
True despair for the jobless is not even looking to see
if your answering machine is blinking.

FREELANCING
Bathrobe work

FREE ENTERPRISE
Free enterprise is when the boss expects you to show enterprise for free.

ON TIME
Getting to work on time makes the day so long.

POOR
You're poor if you hate months with 31 days in them.

'INTERESTING'
'Interesting' is the most damning thing you can say
about someone's work.

PAYDAY
Everyone comes to work on payday.

WORTH
You're not paid what you're worth.
You're paid what you can demand.

WE'RE JUST GETTING THE KNACK OF LIFE
WHEN WE DIE

AGE AND HEALTH

BIRTHDAYS

When we're young, birthdays are a time for celebration.
When we're old, cerebration.

BIOS AND OBITS

How soon our bio becomes our obit.

FORGETFULNESS

Old people aren't forgetful. They've just learned
that most things aren't worth remembering.

HABITS

Drink and smoke and have a stroke.

MELLOWING

Mellowing and burning out are the same thing.

MIDDLE AGE

You're middle-aged when you don't like snow.
You're middle-aged when you bring a chair to the beach.
You're middle-aged when a teenager offers you a seat on
the subway. (You're old when a grownup does).
You're middle-aged when you learn something new
every day -- but forget two or three.

OLD AGE

At 50 you go to reunions.
At 60 you got to wakes.
At 70 you don't go anywhere. You sit home
and watch television.
At 80 you're not even you anymore.

EARLY RISERS

Old people get up early - they're afraid of missing something.

SPRING IS A PROMISE SUMMER DOESN'T KEEP

TIME AND THE SEASONS

CHIMNEYS

In winter, chimneys flaunt white flags from every rooftop.

MAY GLORY

A dead-seeming shrub has its sudden moment
of glory in May, then slumbers again for a year.

MONTHS

October is all Halloween.
November is all Thanksgiving.
December is all Christmas.
January -- forget January.

NEW YEAR

The new year doesn't start on New Year's Day. It starts on the first
Monday after New Year's Day. The second half of the year doesn't
start on Labor Day. It starts on the Monday after Labor Day.

SNOW
A little snow is pretty. A lot is . . . .

SPRING SIGN
Deep in February snow, shop windows have an April glow.

SPRING
The first day of spring is when the girls take their coats off.

SUMMER
Despite all its discomforts, we're sad when summer goes.
It's the bloom of the year, the rest all decay and burial.

TWILIGHT
Twilight is when the young go out to play and the old
go home to collapse.

WEATHER
The weather watches the calendar. Look for sudden changes
on key holidays like Memorial Day and Labor Day.

WEEKENDS

Everything happens on the weekends when there's no one around to fix it.

TO LIVE IS TO DANCE

THE ARTS

CHARACTERS

A character in a play or novel has to be interesting, not necessarily admirable. Richard II and III come to mind.

DRAMA AND FICTION

Character is more important than story. Characters drive the story.

We read *Hamlet* the play for Hamlet the character, not for the absurd story.

EPIGRAMS

An epigram is a distilled novel.

An epigram is a *mot* to trouble the mind's eye.

SENTENCES

One sentence of good fiction is worth 50 pages of introduction by some dull professor.

SINATRA

A nightingale on a dungheap

VENUS DE MILO

A statue of limitations

'WAR AND PEACE'

Without Napoleon, 'War and Peace' would have been as
boring as 'Anna Karenina,' which even Tolstoy found tedious.

WRITERS

A great novel or play must have a great character.
Only a great writer can create one.

WRITERS OUT OF WORK

Lumpen intelligentsia

THE ELECTIONS ARE FREE
BUT THE POLITICIANS ARE EXPENSIVE

POLITICS AND HISTORY

BLOOD

America is the bloodiest country in history, and Americans don't even know it.The bloodletting started with slavery and the wipeout of the indigenous and moved right up to Hiroshima, Vietnam and Libya. Next to us, the Brits and Spanish were pikers. And America has had 400 years for its atrocities. The Nazis only had 12.

CAMPAIGN CONTRIBUTIONS

Campaign contributions aren't a flaw in the system.
Campaign contributions *are* the system.

CLINTON

A cornpone Kennedy in a Dogpatch White House

CLAUSEWITZ

Improving on Clausewitz, who said, 'War is the extension of politics by other means.' Improvement: War is the extension of *economics* by other means. All wars have an economic basis.

COMMUNISM

Communism was a great experiment that failed -- like Christianity.

CONTRADICTION

There is a great contradiction at the heart of what we call democracy: Hopeful voters go to the polls and elect people to local, state and national offices. Those elected go to their offices and immediately become bought-and-paid-for *politicians* - the most despised segment of the population

CUBA

If Cuba announced elections, Karl Rove would be on the next plane to Havana with a suitcase full of thousand-dollar bills.

DICTATORSHIPS

All countries are dictatorships. Some just disguise it better.

ELECTORATES

An electorate travels on its stomach.

HISTORIANS

Mainstream historians are as crooked as mainstream journalists -- purveyors of lies and distortions -- obsessed with keeping their jobs, benefits and tenure.

IMMIGRANTS

Immigrants soon learn the American Way, which is not to read the Federalist Papers from cover to cover and go out and cheer on the Fourth of July. The American Way is to form an association, raise money and buy as many politicians as you can afford.

IMMIGRANTS' PROGRESS

From blue collar to white collar to open collar.

INTERESTS

Regimes and ideologies change, but not interests.

INTERNATIONAL LAW

There's only one international law: Might Makes Right. Tell everything else to children.

INVADERS

Most soldiers in an invading force want only one thing -- to go home. That is their weakness. The people being invaded *are* home. That is their strength.

JOURNALISM

Journalism is public relations with delusions of grandeur.

LEFTISTS

Leftists often look like nuts and losers.
They should hire laid-off stockbrokers as frontmen.

Always be suspicious of fat leftists. Leftists should be lean and hungry, burning with envy and hatred.

LETTERS

What the letters stand for:
CIA: Corporations In Action
FBI: For Business Interests

LAW AND ORDER

One man's law and order is another man's police brutality.
One man's liberation is another man's occupation.

NIETZSCHE

The clown prince of philosophy

PEOPLE

America has gone from a nation of rugged individualists
to a nation of crazed loners.

POWER

Power doesn't need an excuse.

TURNING POINTS

The turning point in Europe in World War II wasn't
Stalingrad in 1942. It was the year before when the German army
ground to a halt outside of Moscow and its troops had to spend the
freezing Russian winter fighting vainly in lightweight uniforms against
counterattacking Soviet troops.

The turning point in the Pacific wasn't Midway. It was Pearl Harbor when the Japanese attacked the much stronger U.S., thereby committing suicide.

Hitler then declared war on the U.S., forcing himself to fight an unwinnable two-front war.

MONEY
Politics always come down to money -- who has it, who wants it, who gets it.

MORALITY
Retired politicians can take moral stands on issues because they don't have to run for office any more. They can offend anyone they want.

POLITICIANS
Politicians: One year they're inducted, next year they're indicted.

POLITICS
Politics is the art of persuading the various classes and ethnic groups to live together without too much violence.

Politics is simply a matter of ins and outs.:
The ins want to *stay* in, the outs want to *get* in.

RELIGION

Religion plus politics equals blood.

REPUBLICANS

Republicans love wars - very profitable for their corporate sponsors.
But they don't like veterans - all those expensive hospitals.

REMINGTON RAMBOS

Tough-guy writers who can't wait for someone else to go to war.

RIGHTS

The only real right is the right of might -- one you can force others
to observe. A right that is granted can be withdrawn.

SNEAK ATTACKS

One man's sneak attack is another man's stroke of tactical genius.

STATESMEN

At heart, every statesmen is a businessman. He wants peace between nations so he can sell them something.

Nations deal with each other through political and military means. The diplomat is merely the broker. If things go well at the conference table, freighters appear at ports. If things go badly, bombers appear overhead.

TERRORISM

Terrorism is what they do to us. Peacekeeping is what we do to them.

WASHINGTON MONUMENT

Are the cracks in the Washington Monument an omen - an augury of a collapsing empire? A broken economy, two lost wars. Not good.